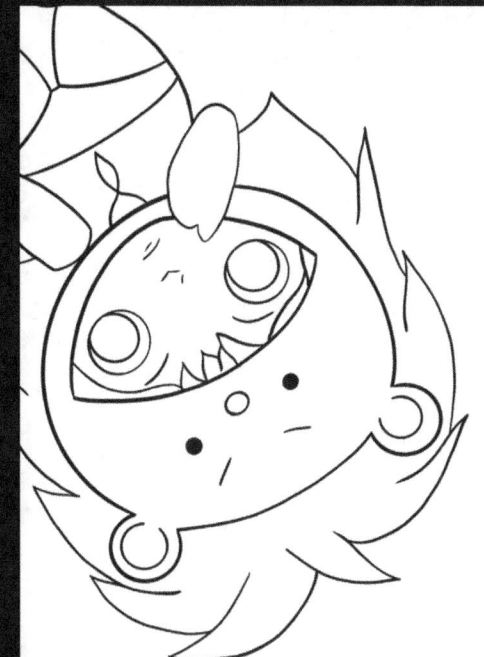

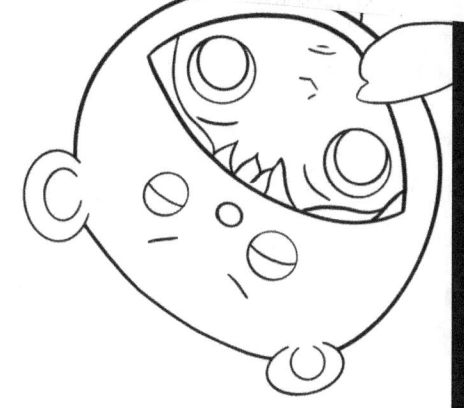

THIS BOOK BELONGS TO:

_____

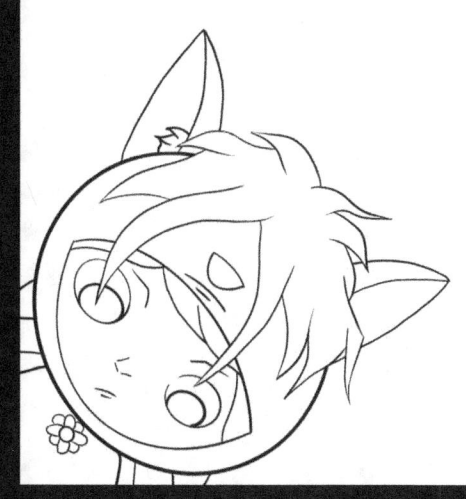
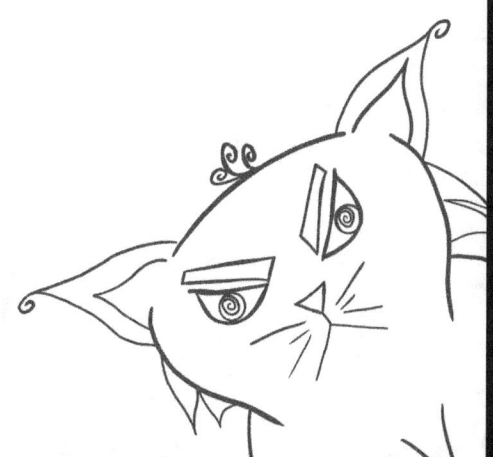

MANDO

Mando

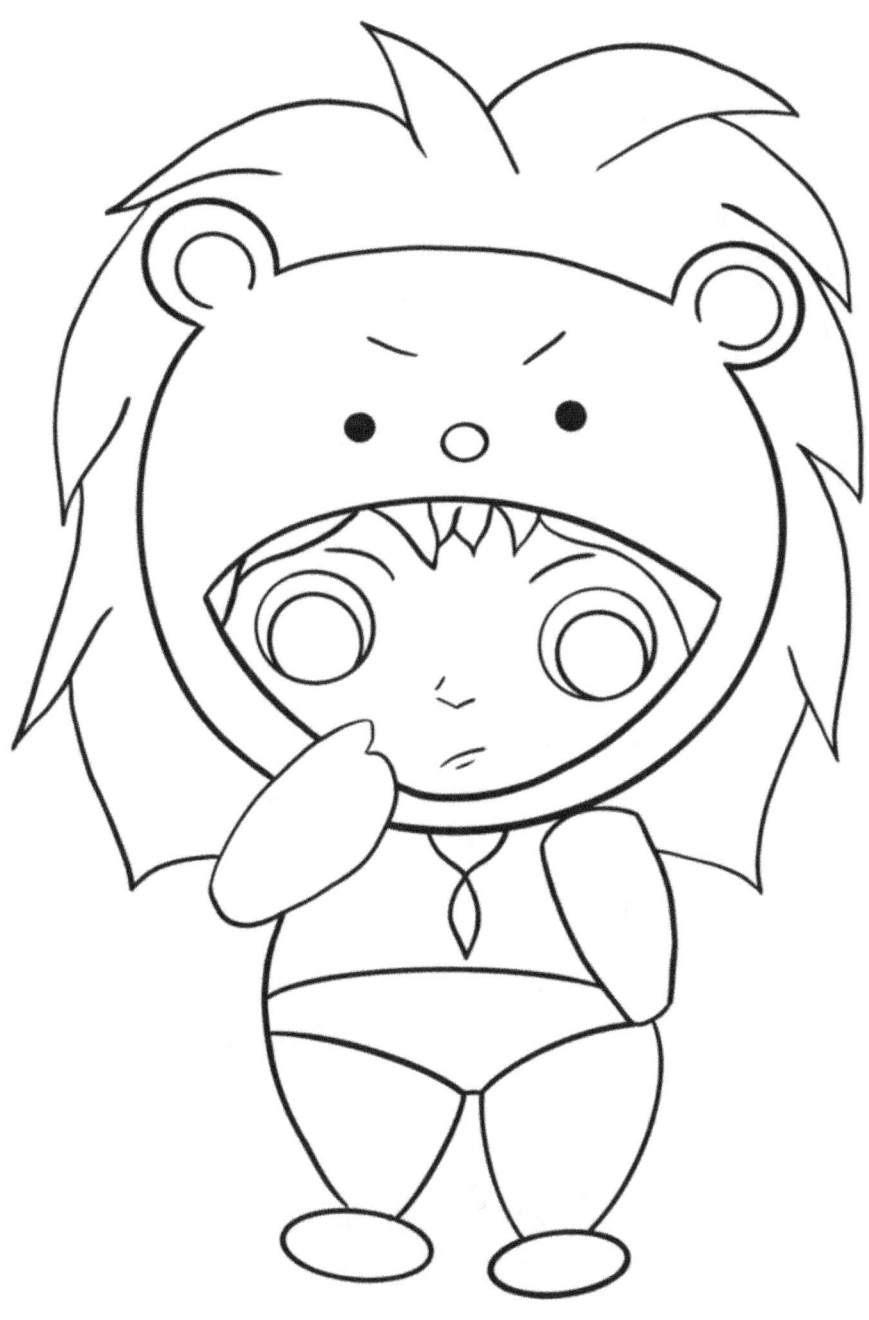

NEO

Neo

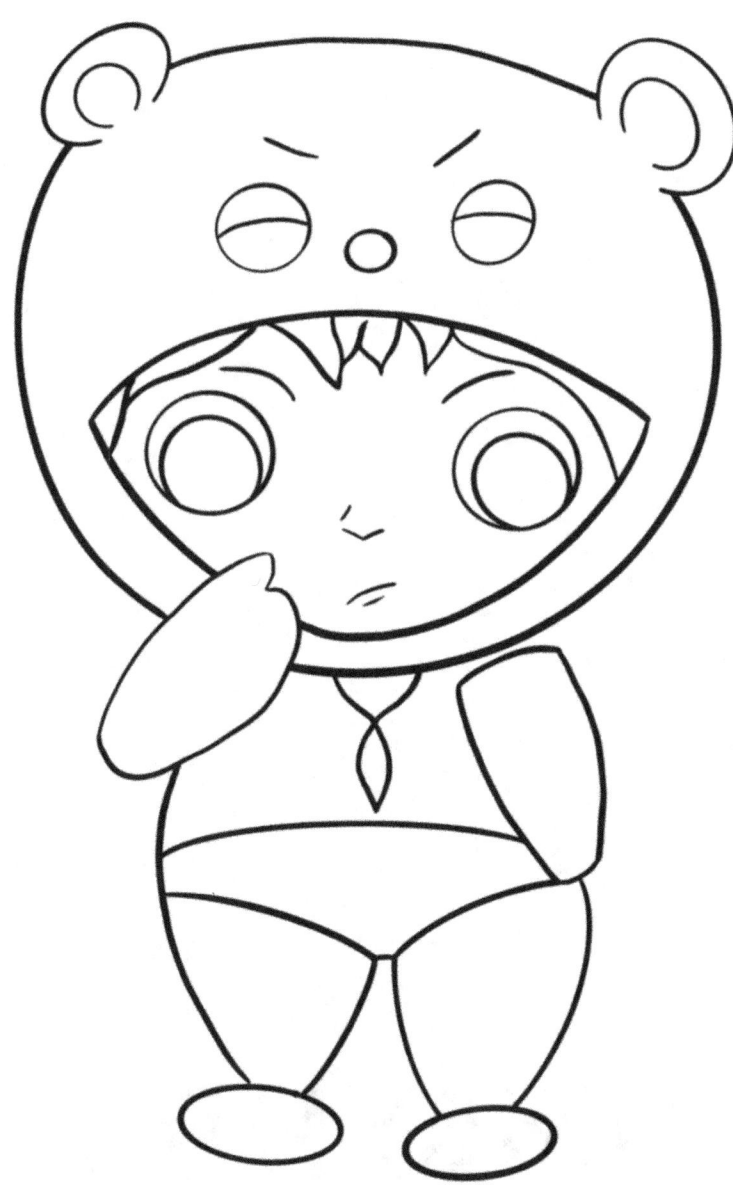

LOLYMAR

LOLYMAR

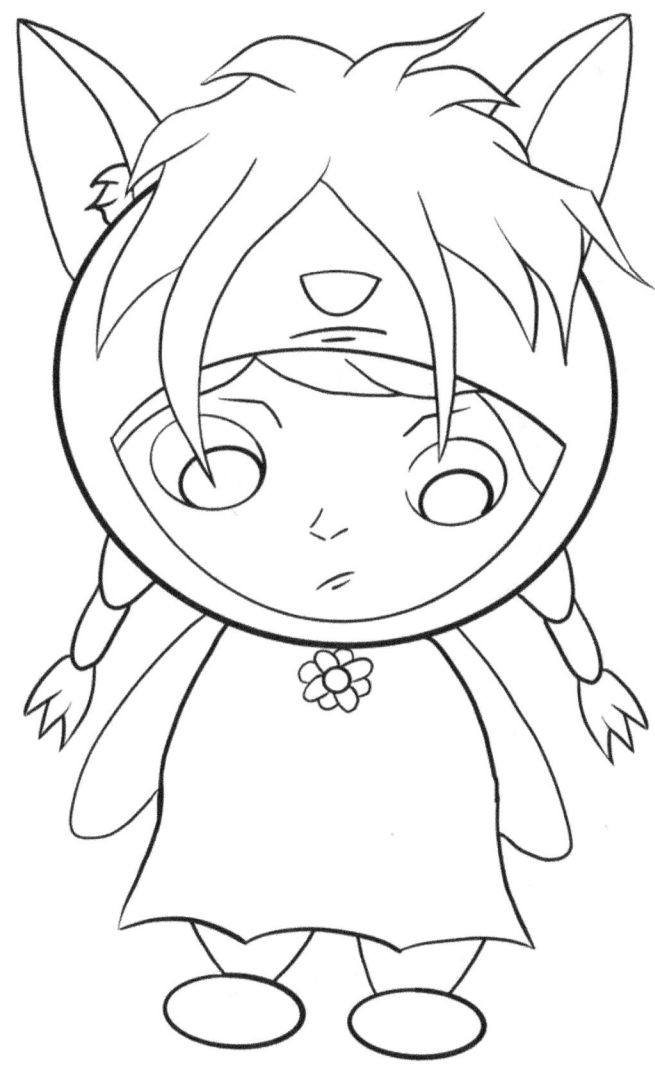

PANDORA

Pandora

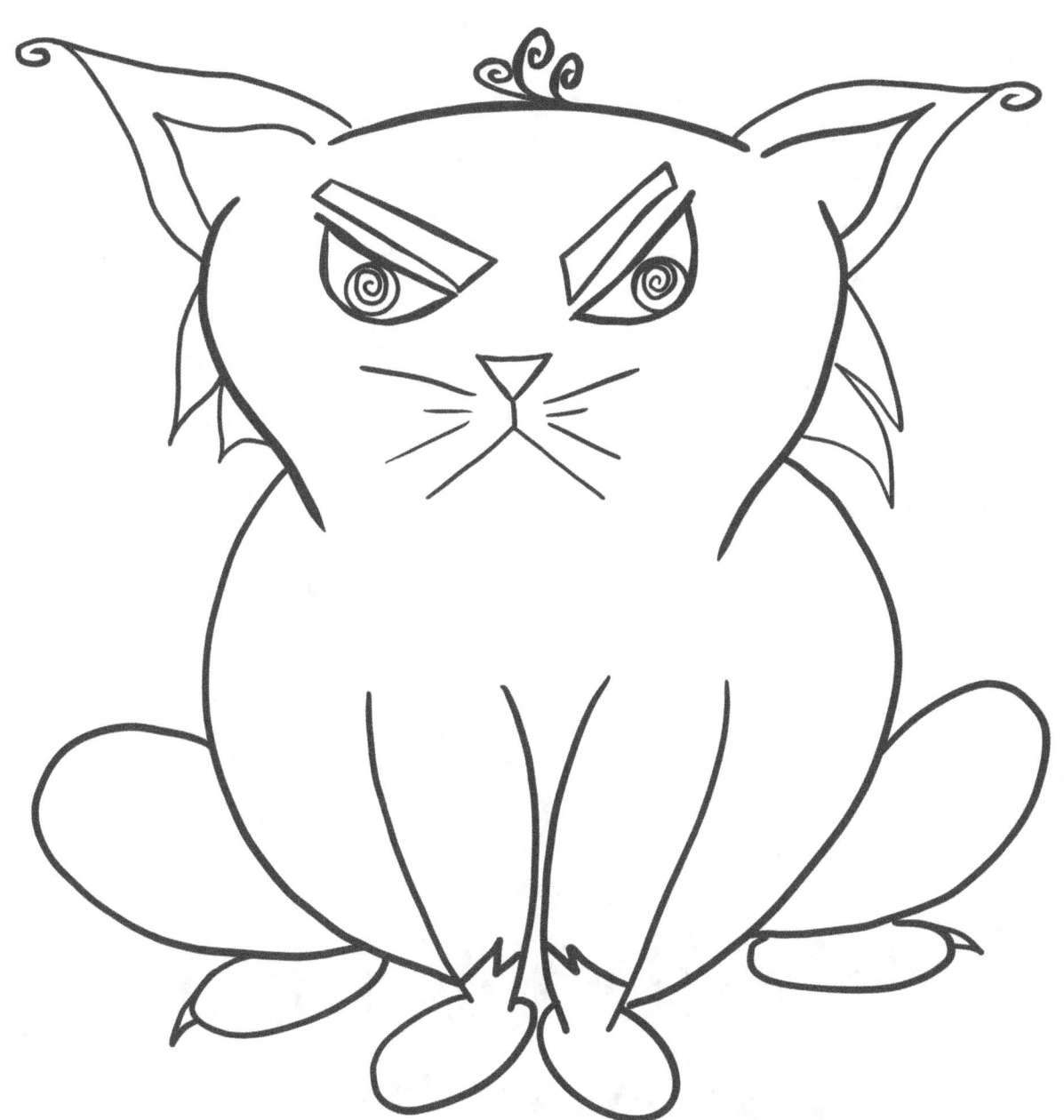

MANDO & NEO
GO DRIVING

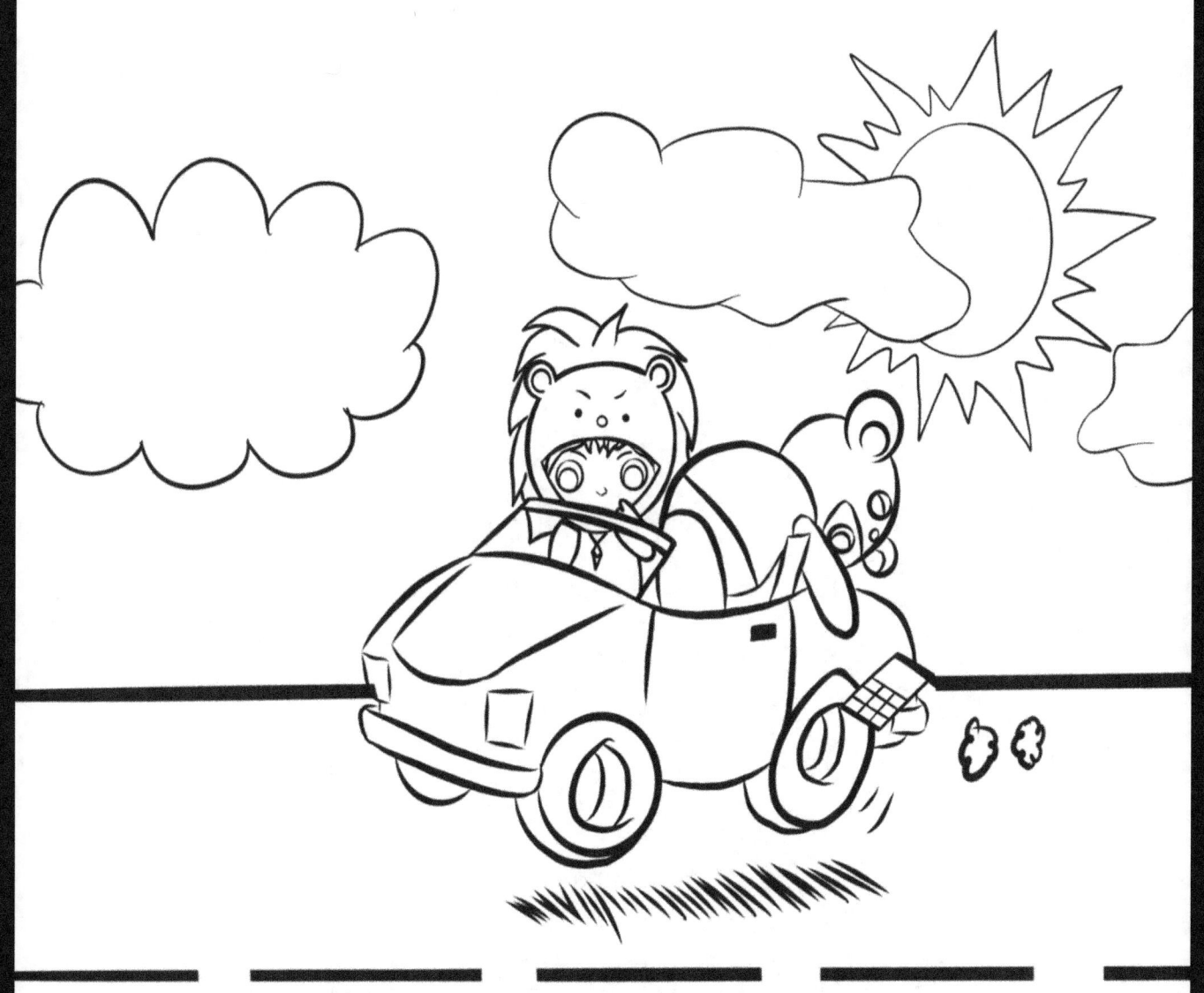

MANDO & NEO
GO TO THE BEACH

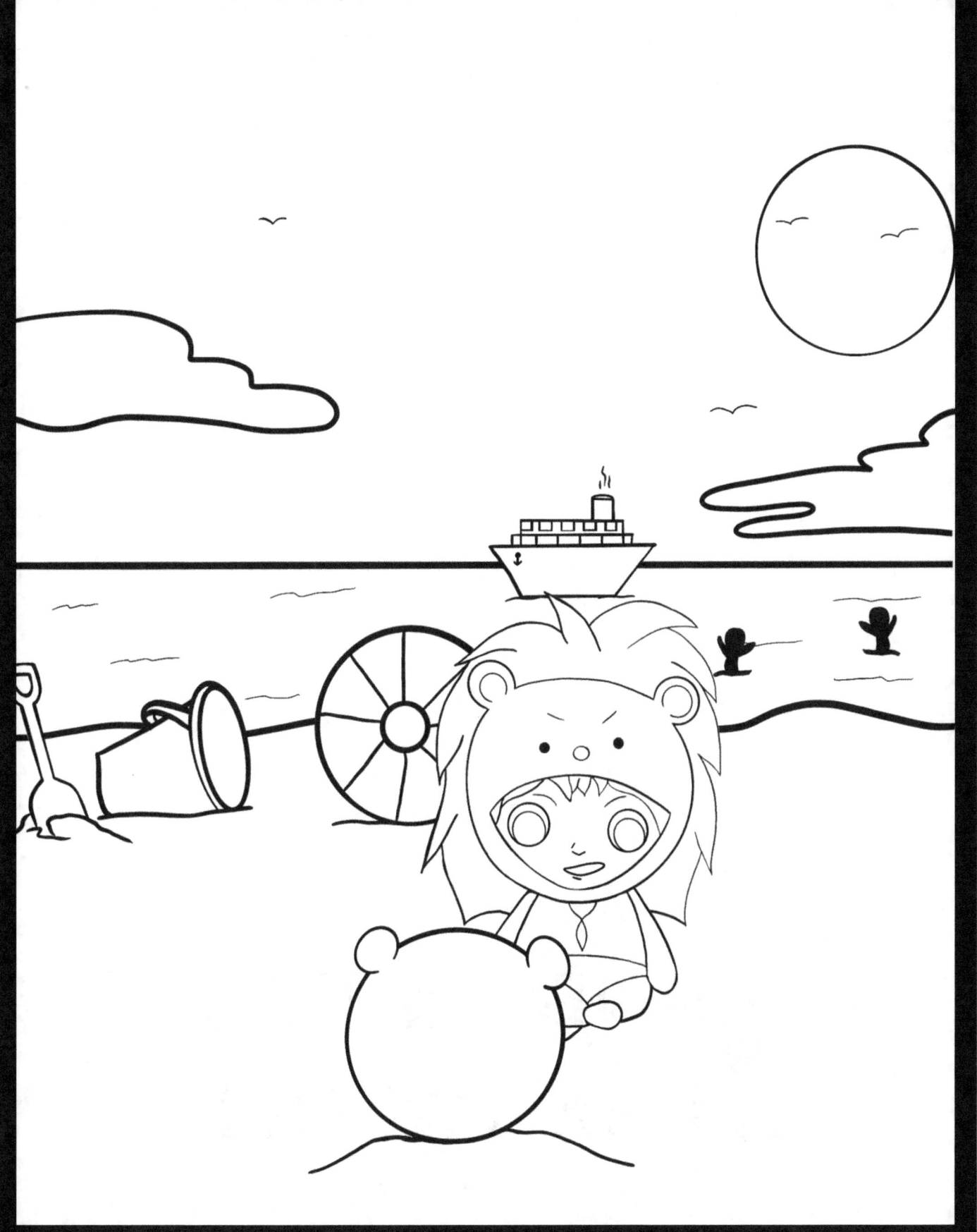

MANDO & NEO
AT SEAWORLD

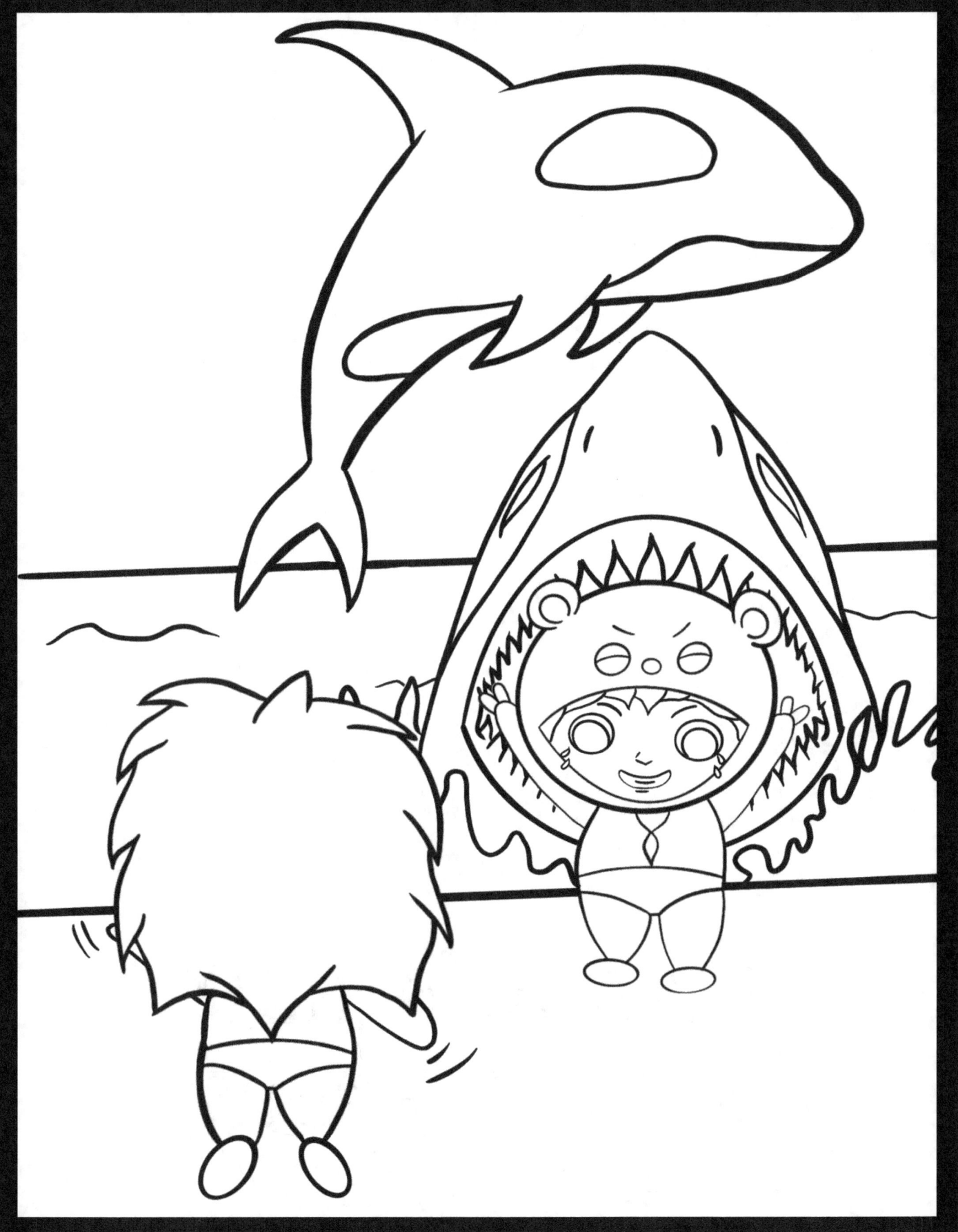

MANDO & NEO
AT THE PARK

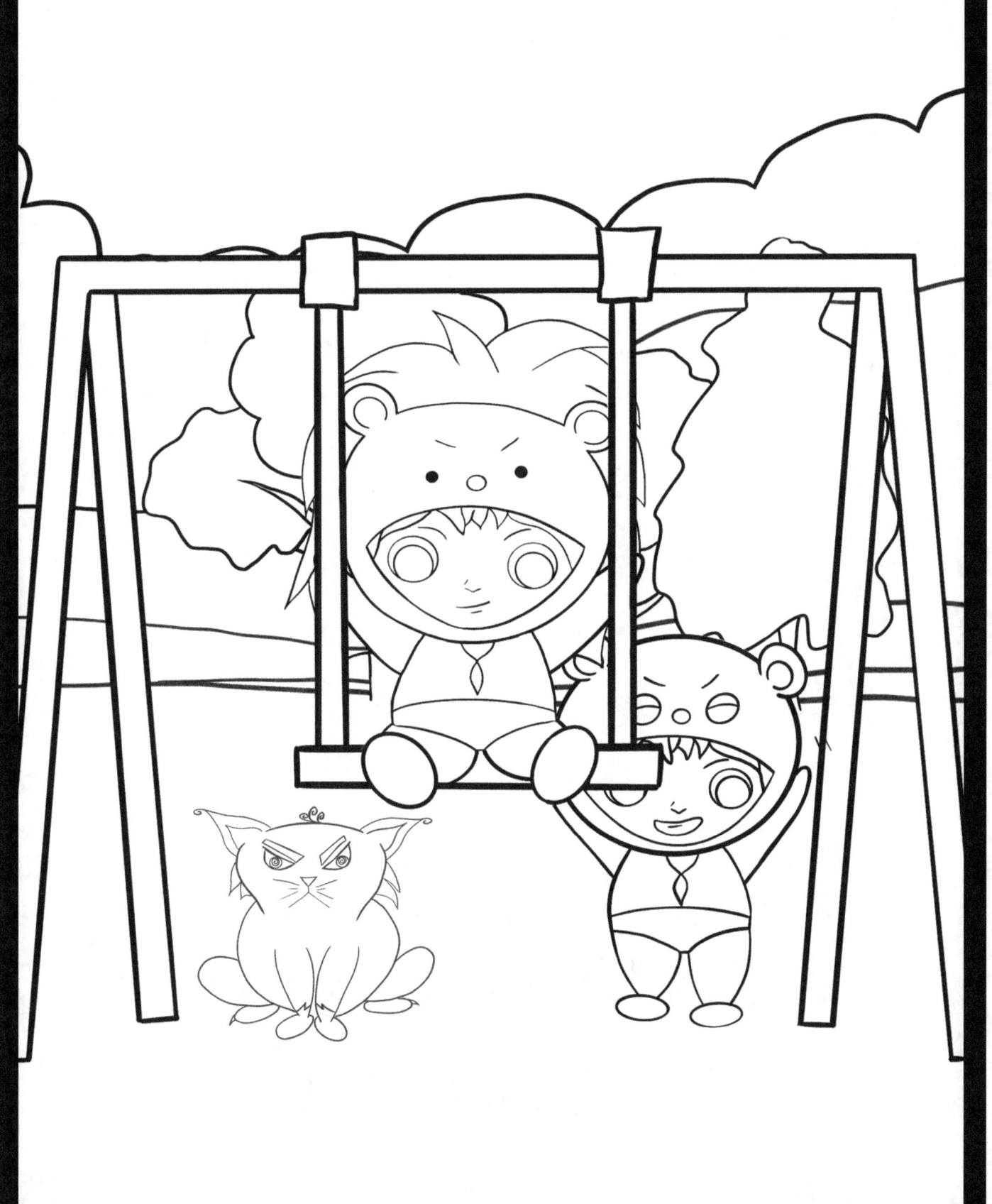

MANDO & NEO AT THE ZOO

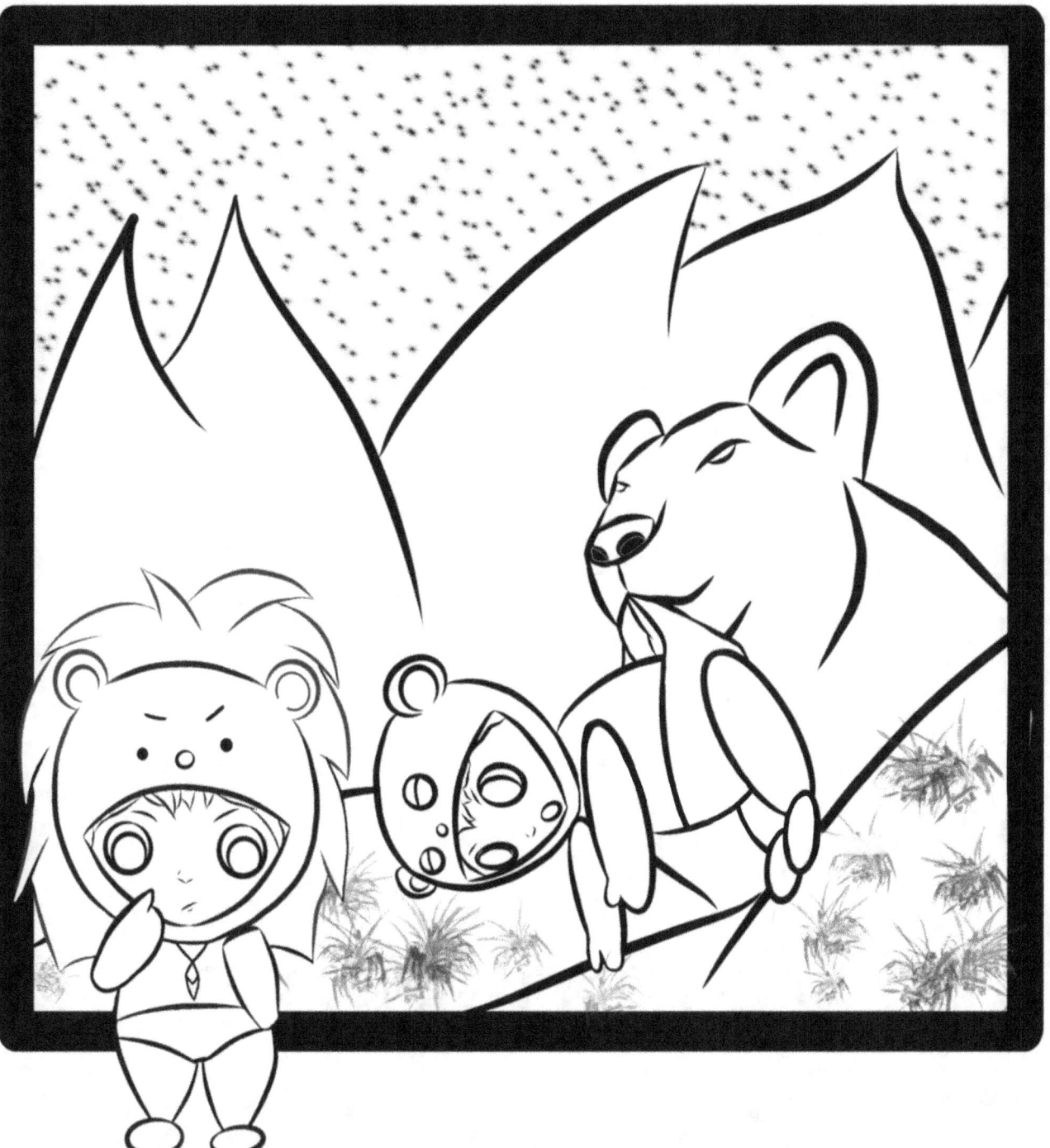

MANDO & NEO
AT A ROLLERCOASTER

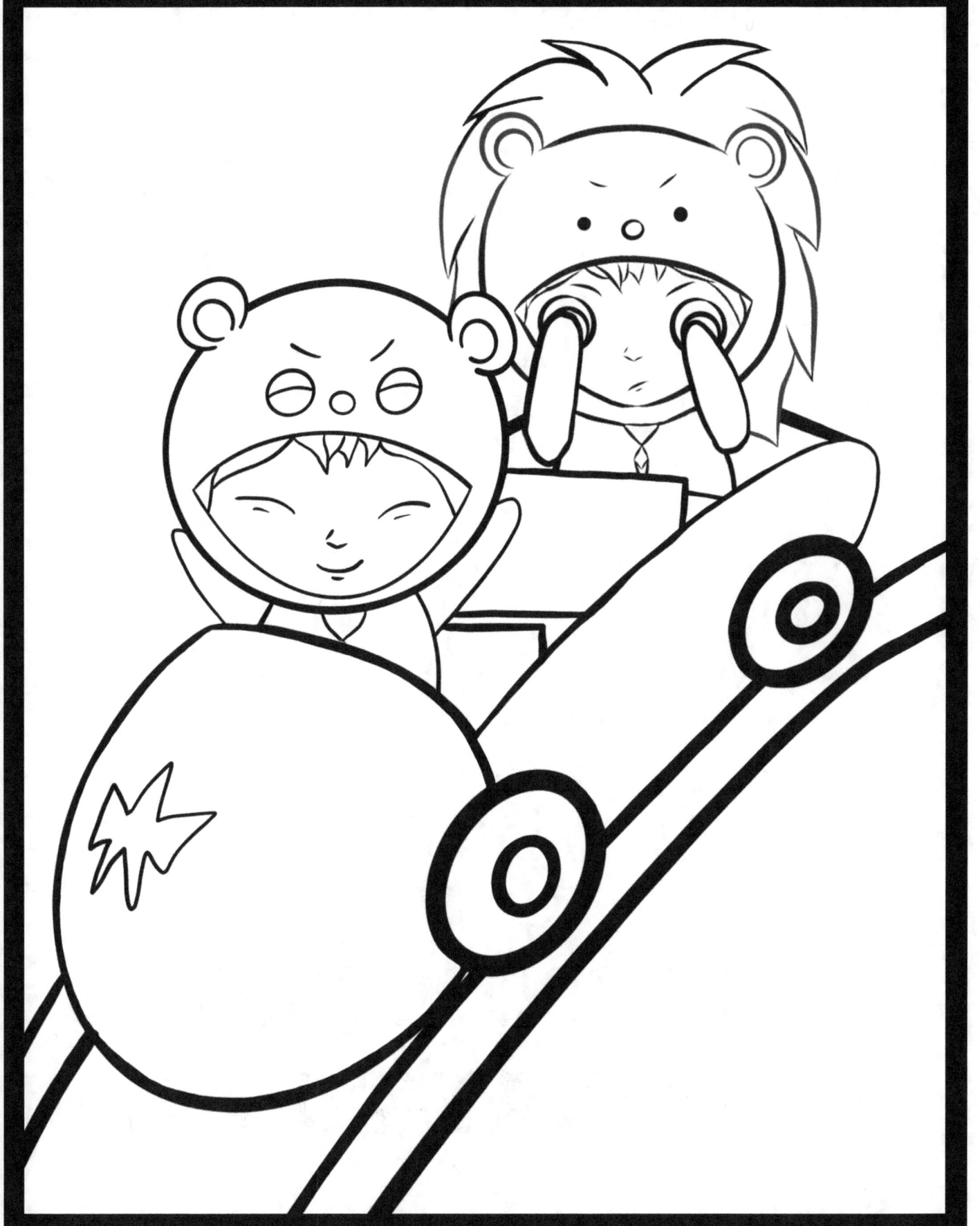

MANDO & NEO
GO DANCING

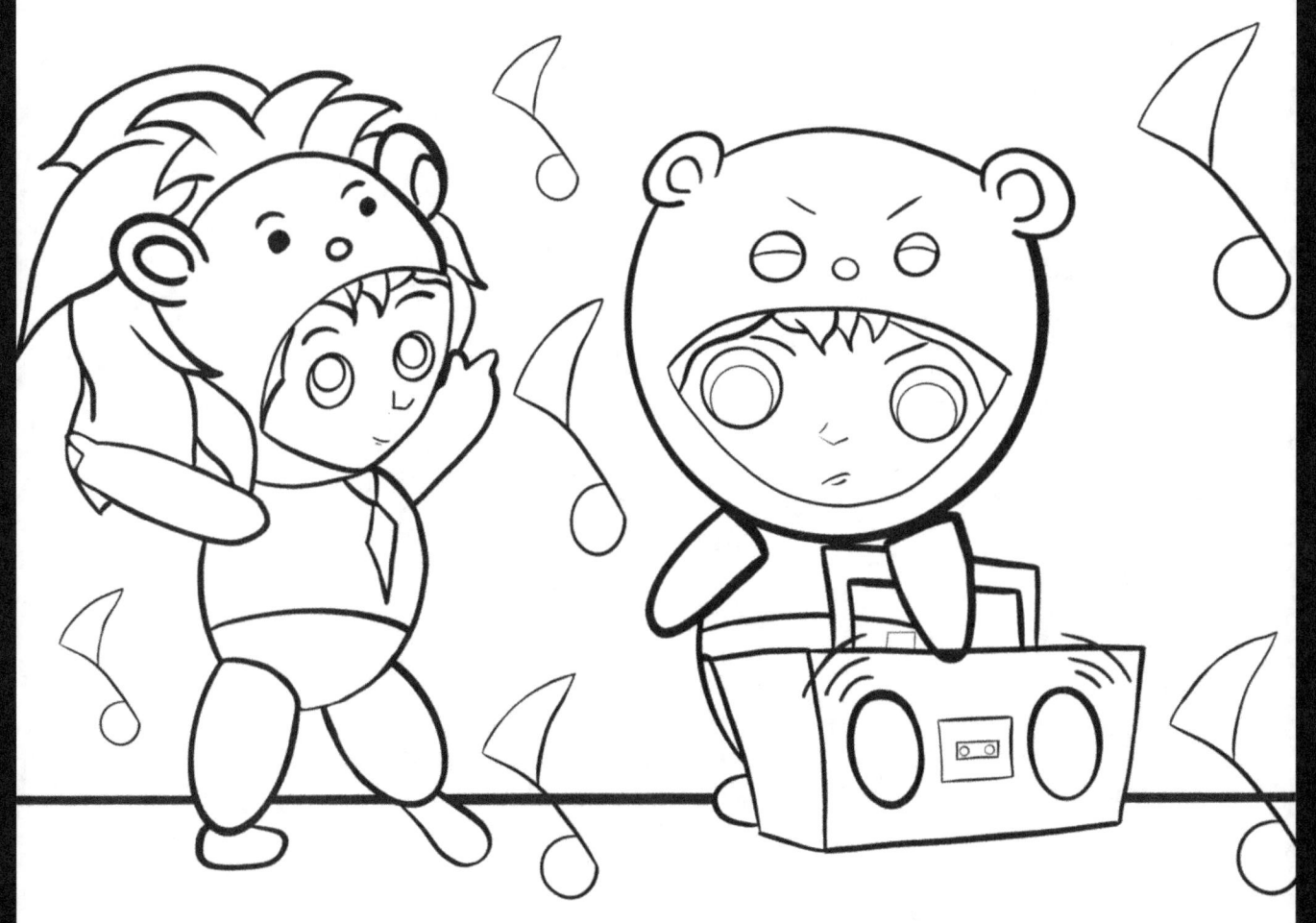

HAPPY BIRTHDAY NEO

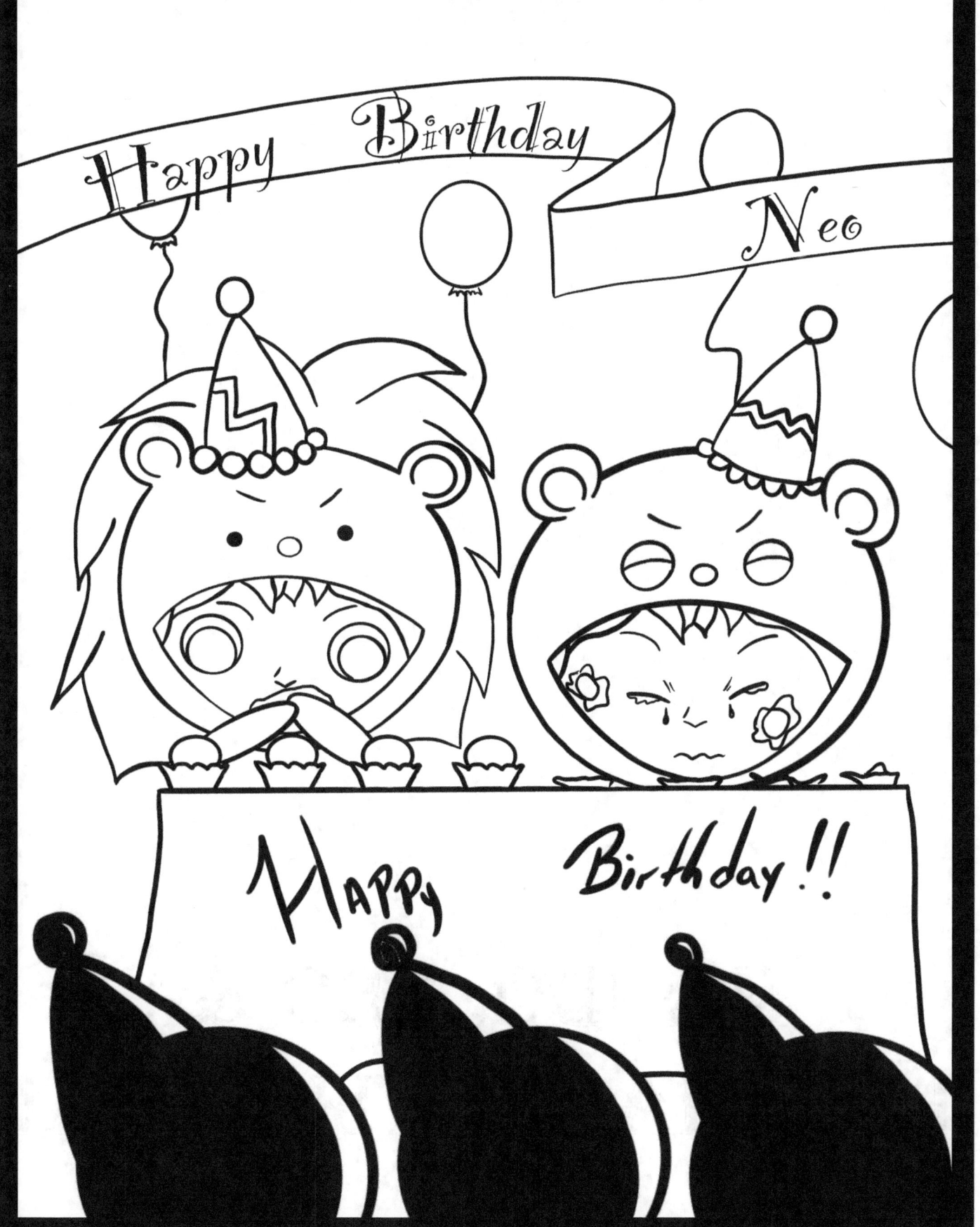

MANDO, NEO & LOLYMAR AT THE GYM

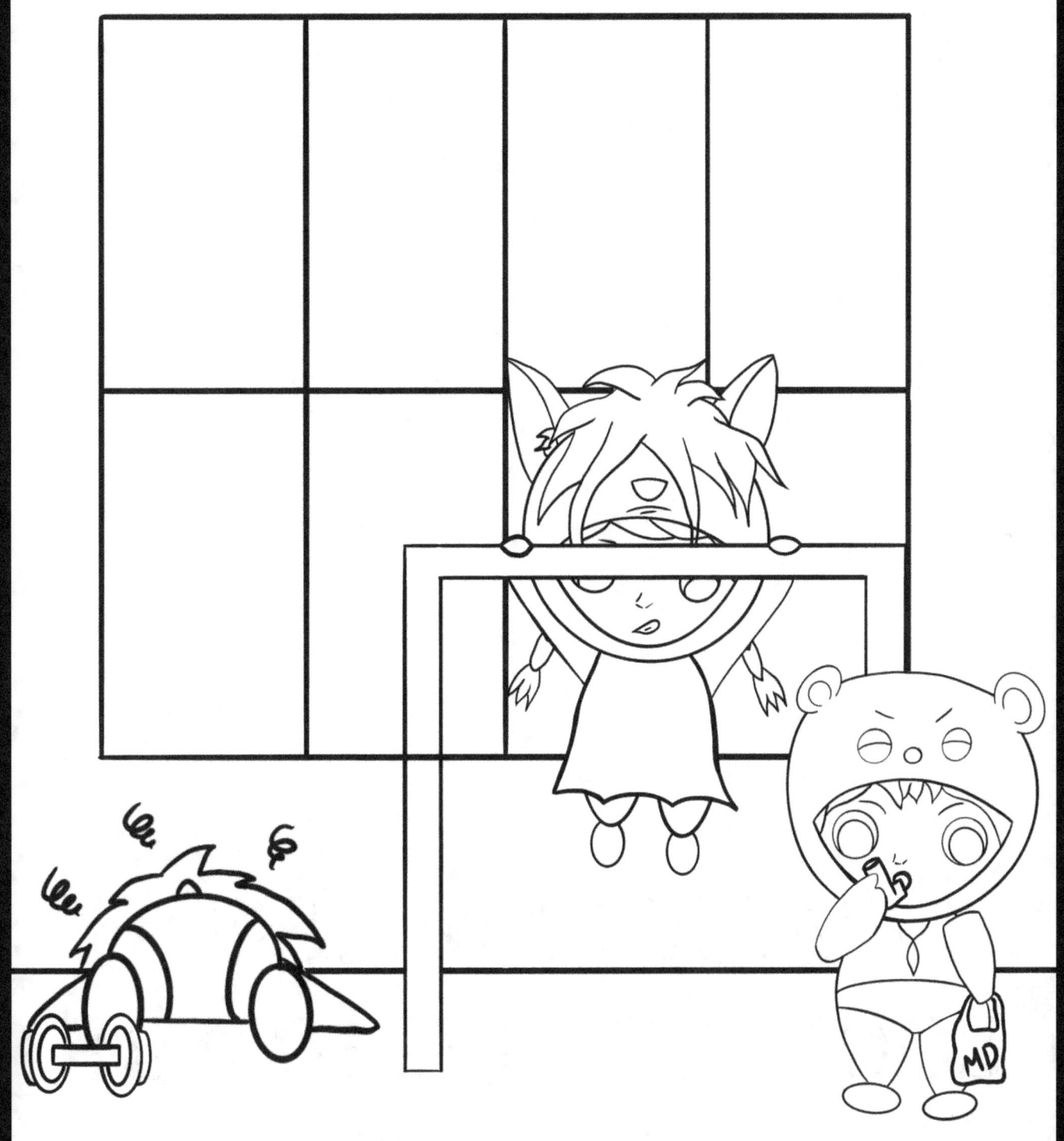

MANDO & NEO
LOOK AT THE STARS

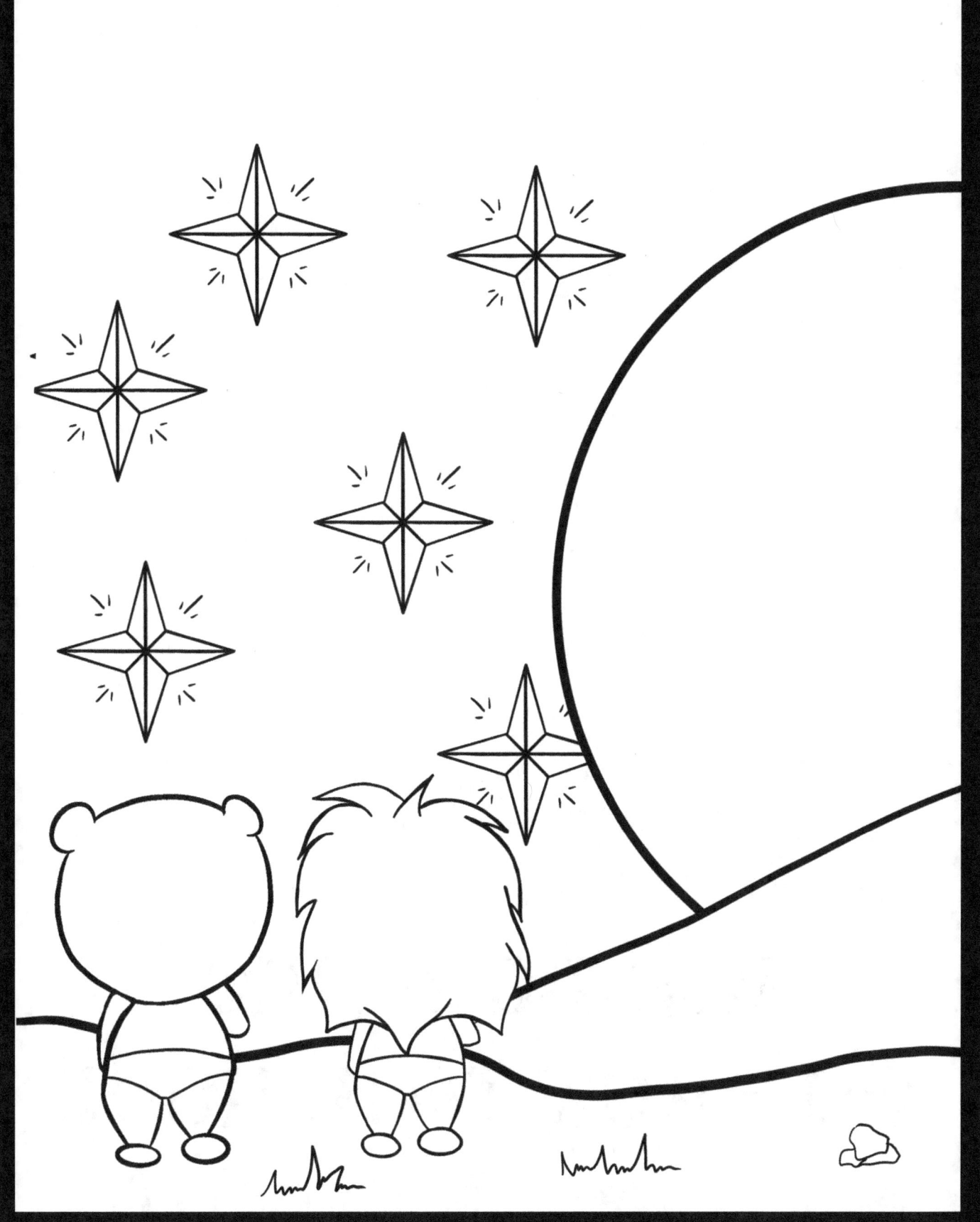

MANDO & NEO
GO BACK TO SCHOOL

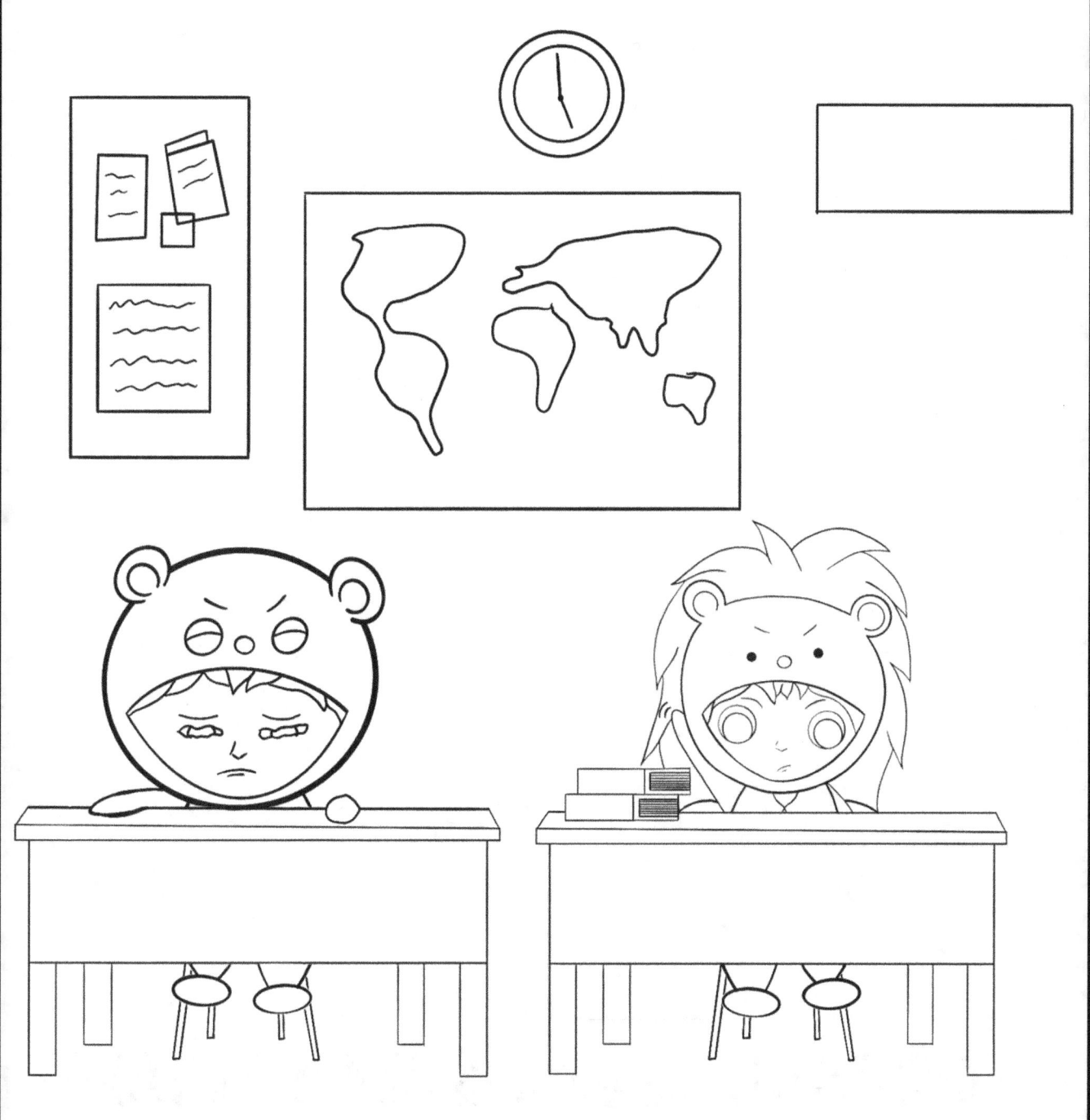

MANDO & NEO GO ON A CRAZY ADVENTURE
BY, ARMANDO CHEVEREZ

www.ingramcontent.com/pod-product-compliance
Lightning Source LLC
Chambersburg PA
CBHW081100240526

45465CB00025B/2793